100 Things
you should know about
Bugs

100 Things
you should know about
Bugs

Steve Parker

Consultant: Dr. Jim Flegg

MASON CREST PUBLISHERS INC.
370 Reed Road
Broomall, Pennsylvania 19008
(866)MCP-BOOK (toll free)
www.masoncrest.com

ISBN: 978-1-4222-1967-6
Series ISBN (15 titles): 978-1-4222-1964-5

First Printing
9 8 7 6 5 4 3 2 1

Cataloging-in-Publication Data on file with the Library of Congress.
Printed in the U.S.A.

First published as hardback in 2001 by Miles Kelly Publishing Ltd
Bardfield Centre, Great Bardfield, Essex, CM7 4SL

Editorial Director: Belinda Gallagher

Art Director: Jo Brewer

Editor: Neil de Cort

Assistant Editor: Lucy Dowling

Volume Designer: Sally Lace

Picture Researcher: Liberty Newton

Proofreader: Janet De Saulles

Indexer: Jane Parker

Production Manager: Elizabeth Brunwin

Reprographics: Anthony Cambray, Stephan Davis,
Liberty Newton, Ian Paulyn

Editions Manager: Bethan Ellish

All images from the Miles Kelly Archives

Contents

Insects or spiders?

1 **Insects are among the most numerous and widespread animals on Earth.** They form the largest of all animal groups, with millions of different kinds, or species, that live almost everywhere in the world. But not all creepy-crawlies are insects. Spiders belong to a different group called arachnids, and millipedes are in yet another group!

Tortoiseshell butterfly

Spiny green nymph

Cricket

Pink-winged stick insect

Tarantula

Cockchafer beetle

Stag beetle

Dragonfly

Honeybee

Honeybee

Tarantula hawk wasp

Millipede

Giant longhorn beetle

Wood ants

Insects everywhere!

2 The housefly is one of the most common, widespread and annoying insects. There are many other members of the fly group, such as bluebottles, horseflies, craneflies ("daddy-longlegs"), and fruitflies. They all have two wings. Most other kinds of insects have four wings.

Housefly

3 The ladybug is a noticeable insect with its bright red or yellow body and black spots. It is a member of the beetle group. This is the biggest of all insect groups, with more than half a million kinds, from massive goliath and rhinoceros beetles to tiny flea beetles and weevil beetles.

4 The white butterfly is not usually welcome in the garden. Their young, known as caterpillars, eat the leaves of the gardener's precious flowers and vegetables. There are thousands of kinds of butterflies and even more kinds of their night-time cousins, the moths.

White butterfly feeding from a flower

5 The earwig is a familiar insect in the park, garden, garage, shed—and sometimes house. Despite their name, earwigs do not crawl into ears or hide in wigs. But they do like dark, damp corners. Earwigs form one of the smaller insect groups, with only 1,300 different kinds.

◀ This earwig is being threatened, so it raises its tail to try to make itself look bigger.

6 Ants are fine in the garden or wood, but are pests in the house. Ants, bees and wasps make up a large insect group with some 300,000 different kinds. Most can sting, although many are too small to hurt people. However, some, such as bulldog ants, have a painful bite.

SPOT THE INSECTS!

Have you seen any insects so far today? Maybe a fly whizzing around the house or a butterfly flitting among the flowers? On a warm summer's day you probably see many kinds of insects. On a cold winter's day there are fewer insects around. Most are hiding away or have not yet hatched out of their eggs.

◀ Insects like these white butterflies do not have a bony skeleton inside their bodies like we do. Their bodies are covered by a series of horny plates called an exoskeleton.

7 The scorpionfly has a nasty looking sting on a long curved tail. It flies or crawls in bushes and weeds during summer. Only the male scorpionfly has the red tail. It looks like the sting of a scorpion but is harmless.

How insects grow

8 **All insects begin life inside an egg.** The female insect usually lays her eggs in an out-of-the-way place, such as under a stone, leaf or bark, or in the soil.

▲ This female stag beetle does not have huge jaws for fighting like the male does. However, her bite is much more powerful than the male's.

9 **When some types of insects hatch, they do not look like their parents.** A young beetle, butterfly, or fly is very different from a grown-up beetle, butterfly, or fly. It is soft-bodied, wriggly, and wormlike. This young stage is called a larva. There are different names for various kinds of larvae. A fly larva is called a maggot, a beetle larva is a grub, and a butterfly larva is a caterpillar.

10 **A female insect mates with a male insect before she can lay her eggs.** The female and male come together to check that they are both the same kind of insect, and they are both healthy and ready to mate. This is known as courtship. Butterflies often flit through the air together in a "courtship dance."

▶ Large caterpillars always eat into the center of the leaf from the edge. Caterpillars grasp the leaf with their legs, while their specially developed front jaws chew at their food.

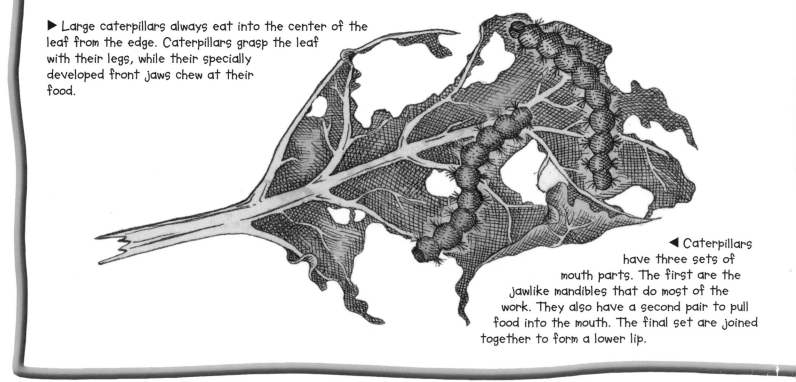

◀ Caterpillars have three sets of mouth parts. The first are the jawlike mandibles that do most of the work. They also have a second pair to pull food into the mouth. The final set are joined together to form a lower lip.

Pupa

11 The larva eats and eats. It sheds its skin several times so it can grow. Then it changes into the next stage of its life, called a pupa. The pupa has a hard outer case which stays still and inactive. But, inside, the larva is changing body shape again. This change of shape is known as metamorphosis.

▲ This peacock butterfly has just emerged from its pupal case and is stretching its wings for the first time.

12 At last the pupa's case splits open and the adult insect crawls out. Its body, legs, and wings spread out and harden. Now the insect is ready to find food and also find a mate.

13 Some kinds of insects change shape less as they grow up. When a young cricket or grasshopper hatches from its egg, it looks similar to its parents. However, it may not have any wings yet.

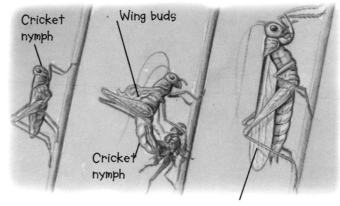

Cricket nymph

Wing buds

Cricket nymph

Mature adult

14 The young cricket eats and eats, and sheds or molts its skin several times as it grows. Each time it looks more like its parent. A young insect which resembles the fully grown adult like this is called a nymph. At the last molt it becomes a fully formed adult, ready to feed and breed.

I DON'T BELIEVE IT!
Courtship is a dangerous time for the hunting insect called the praying mantis. The female is much bigger than the male, and as soon as they have mated, she may eat him!

Air aces

15 Most kinds of insects have two pairs of wings and use them to fly from place to place. One of the strongest fliers is the Apollo butterfly of Europe and Asia. It flaps high over hills and mountains, then rests on a rock or flower in the sunshine.

16 A fast and fierce flying hunter is the dragonfly. Its huge eyes spot tiny prey such as midges and mayflies. The dragonfly dashes through the air, turns in a flash, grabs the victim in its legs and whirs back to a perch to eat its meal.

17 Some insects flash bright lights as they fly. The firefly is not a fly but a type of beetle. Male fireflies "dance" in the air at dusk, the rear parts of their bodies glowing on and off about once each second. Female fireflies stay on twigs and leaves and glow in reply as part of their courtship.

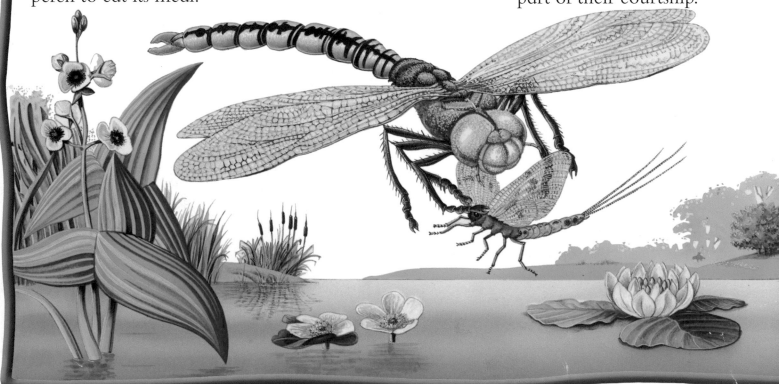

18 The smallest fliers include gnats, midges, and mosquitoes. These are all true flies, with one pair of wings. Some are almost too tiny for us to see. Certain types bite animals and people, sucking their blood as food.

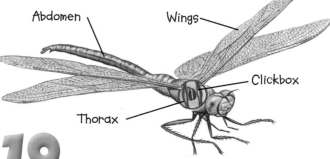

Abdomen

Wings

Clickbox

Thorax

19 An insect's wings are attached to the middle part of its body, the thorax. This is like a box with strong walls, called a clickbox. Muscles inside the thorax pull to make the walls click in and out, which makes the wings flick up and down. A large butterfly flaps its wings once or twice each second. Some tiny flies flap almost 1,000 times each second.

MAKE A FLAPPING FLY

You will need

some stiff cardboard   round-ended scissors
tissue paper   tape

1. Ask an adult for help. Carefully cut the cardboard to make a box with two open ends as shown.

2. Use strips of stiff cardboard to make struts for the wings and attach these to the side walls of the box. Make the rest of the wings from tissue paper.

3. Hold the box as shown. Move the top and bottom walls in, then out. This bends the side walls and makes the wings flap, just like a real insect.

20 A few insects lack wings. They are mostly very small and live in the soil, such as bristletails and springtails. One kind of bristletail is the silverfish—a small, shiny, fast-running insect.

Champion leapers

21 **Many insects move around mainly by hopping and jumping, rather than flying.** They have long, strong legs and can leap great distances, especially to avoid enemies and escape from danger. Grasshoppers are up to 6 inches (15 centimeters) long. Most have very long back legs and some types can jump more than 10 feet (3 meters). Often the grasshopper opens its brightly patterned wings briefly as it leaps, giving a flash of color.

Grasshopper

22 **The champion leaping insects, for their body size, are fleas.** They are mostly small, just 0.1 inch (2-3 millimeters) long. But they can jump over a foot (30 centimeters), which is more than 100 times their body size. Fleas suck blood or body fluids from warm-blooded animals, mainly mammals but also birds.

23
An insect leaper that jumps with its tail, rather than its legs, is the springtail. Springtails are tiny, 0.1 inch (2-3 millimeters) long, or as long as this letter "l"! Some types can leap more than 2 inches (5 centimeters).

24
The click beetle, or skipjack, is another insect leaper. This beetle is about 0.5 inch (12 millimeters) long. When in danger it falls on its back and pretends to be dead. But it slowly arches its body and then straightens with a jerk and a "click." It can flick itself about 10 inches (25 centimeters) into the air!

QUIZ

Which type of insect can jump farthest?

Put these insects in order of how far they can leap.
Grasshopper   Flea
Click beetle   Springtail

Now put them in order of how far they can leap compared to their sizes.

The grasshopper can jump farthest, then the flea, click beetle and finally the springtail. The flea can jump farthest for its size, then the click beetle, the springtail and finally the grasshopper.

Click beetle

▲ The "tail" rear part of the springtail's body, is shaped like a V or Y. It is usually folded under the body and held in place by a triggerlike flap. When the flap moves aside the "tail" flicks down and flips the insect through the air.

Super sprinters

25 Some insects rarely fly or leap. They prefer to run, and run, and run… all day, and even all night too. Among the champion insect runners are cockroaches. They are tough and adaptable, with about 3,600 different kinds. A few burrow in soil or live in caves. But most scurry speedily across the ground on their long legs. They have low, flat bodies and can dart into narrow crevices, under logs and stones and bricks, and into cupboards, furniture— and beds!

Green tiger beetle

26 The green tiger beetle is an active hunter that races over open ground almost too fast for our eyes to follow. It chases smaller creatures such as ants, woodlice, worms, and little spiders. It has huge jaws for its size and soon rips apart any victim.

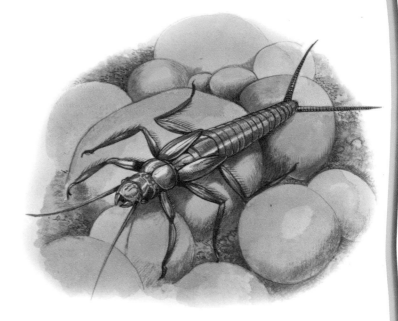

▲ The stonefly nymph, the larva of the stonefly, runs around on the bed of its river home searching for food.

27 One of the busiest insect walkers is the devil's coach horse, a type of beetle with a long body that resembles an earwig. It belongs to the group known as rove beetles which walk huge distances to find food. The devil's coach horse has powerful mouthparts and tears apart dead and dying small caterpillars, grubs, and worms.

Devil's coach horse

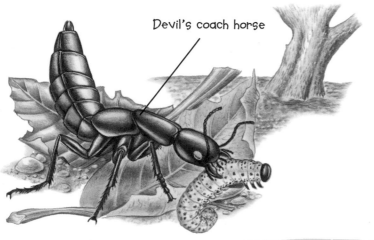

28 Some insects walk not only across the ground, but also up smooth, shiny surfaces such as walls and even windows. They have wide feet with many tiny hooks or sticky pads. These grip bumps that are too small to see in substances such as glossy, wet leaves or window glass.

Stunning swimmers

29 Many kinds of insects live underwater in ponds, streams, rivers, and lakes. Some walk about on the bottom, such as the young forms or nymphs of dragonflies and damselflies. Others swim strongly using their legs as oars to row through the water. The great diving beetle hunts small water creatures such as tadpoles and baby fish. It can give a person a painful bite in self-defense.

30 Some water insects, such as the great silver water beetle, breathe air. So they must come to the surface for fresh supplies. The hairs on the beetle's body trap tiny bubbles of air for breathing below.

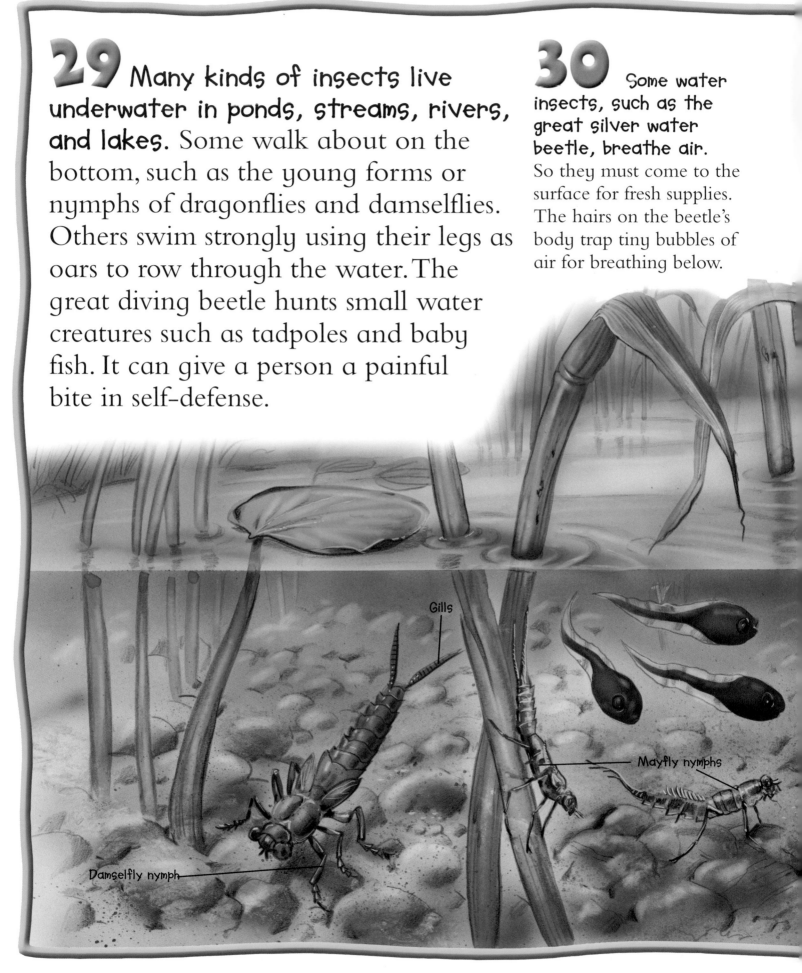

Gills

Mayfly nymphs

Damselfly nymph

31

Some insects even walk on water. The pondskater has a slim, light body with long, wide-splayed legs. It glides across the surface "skin" or film caused by the feature of water known as surface tension. It is a member of the bug group of insects and eats tiny animals that fall into the pond.

32

The nymphs of dragonflies, damselflies, stoneflies, and mayflies have tails with feathery gills. These work like the gills of a fish, for breathing underwater. These young insects never need to go to the surface until they change into adults.

MAKE AN INSECT DIVING SUIT

Young caddisflies, called nymphs, make tube-shaped cases, called caddis cases. These protect the nymph's body underwater. They are made using small bits which the nymph collects from its surroundings. Each caddis uses different bits to make its case. You can make your own caddis case, and you can even choose what sort of caddis you want to be!

With the help of an adult, roll up some pieces of cardboard to make tubes to wear on your forearm. Stick bits on to build giant caddis cases. Make:
a great red sedge caddis of leaves
a silver-horn caddis of pebbles and pieces of sand
Put your arm through a tube and wiggle your fingers like the caddis's head!

Pond skater

Great diving beetle

Dragonfly nymph

Brilliant burrowers

33 Soil teems with millions of creatures—and many are insects. Some are the wormlike young forms of insects, called larvae or grubs, as shown below. Others are fully grown insects, such as burrowing beetles, ants, termites, springtails and earwigs. These soil insects are a vital source of food for all kinds of larger animals from spiders and shrews to moles and many types of birds.

35 The larva of the click beetle is shiny orange, up to an inch (25 millimeters) long and called a wireworm. It stays undergound, feeding on plant parts, for up to five years. Then it changes into an adult and leaves the soil. Wireworms can be serious pests of cereal crops such as barley, oats, and wheat. They also eat beets and potatoes that you would find underground.

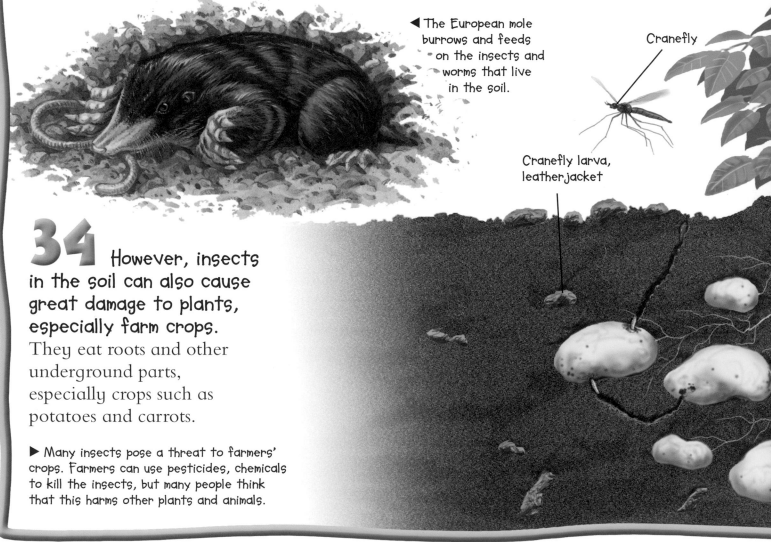

◀ The European mole burrows and feeds on the insects and worms that live in the soil.

Cranefly

Cranefly larva, leatherjacket

34 However, insects in the soil can also cause great damage to plants, especially farm crops. They eat roots and other underground parts, especially crops such as potatoes and carrots.

▶ Many insects pose a threat to farmers' crops. Farmers can use pesticides, chemicals to kill the insects, but many people think that this harms other plants and animals.

36 The larva of the cranefly is called a leatherjacket after its tough, leathery skin. Leatherjackets eat the roots of grasses, including cereal crops such as wheat. They hatch from their eggs in late summer, feed in the soil through autumn and winter and spring, and change into pupae and then adults the next summer.

QUIZ

Sort out the following items into three groups:

A Larger animals that eat insect larvae
B Insect larvae
C Plants eaten by larvae

1. Crow
2. Potato
3. Wireworm
4. Mole
5. Cicada grub
6. Carrot

A. 1 and 4. B. 3 and 5.
C. 2 and 6.

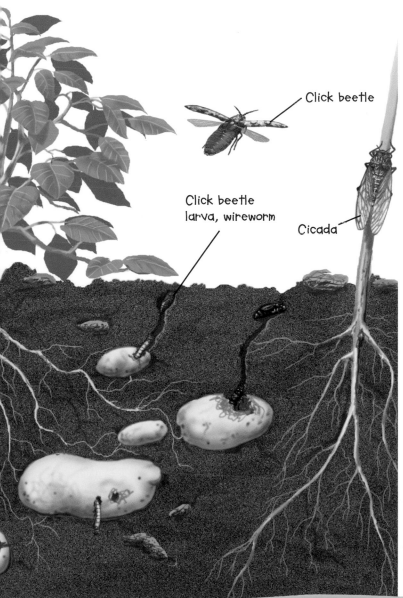

Click beetle

Click beetle larva, wireworm

Cicada

37 The larva of the cicada may live underground for more than ten years. Different types of cicadas stay in the soil for different periods of time. The American periodic cicada is probably the record-holder, taking 17 years to change into a pupa and then an adult. Cicada larvae suck juices from plant roots. Grown-up cicadas make loud chirping or buzzing sounds.

Cicada larva

Bloodthirsty bugs

38 Most insects may be small, but they are among the fiercest and hungriest hunters in the animal world. Many have mouthparts shaped like spears or saws, which are relatively big compared to their bodies, for grabbing and tearing up victims. Some actively chase after prey. Others lie in wait and surprise the prey.

Antenna detects smells

Jaws used for digging and cutting up food

▲ Wasp's head

39 The lacewing looks delicate and dainty as it sits on a leaf by day or flies gently at night. However, it is a fearsome hunter of smaller creatures, especially aphids such as greenfly and blackfly. It chews the aphid and drinks its body fluids. It may also have a sip of sweet, sugary nectar from a flower.

40 One of the most powerful insect predators is the preying mantis. It is also called the praying mantis since it holds its front legs folded, like a person with hands together in prayer. But the front legs have sharp spines and snap together like spiky scissors to grab caterpillars, moths and similar food.

▼ Lacewing eating an aphid.

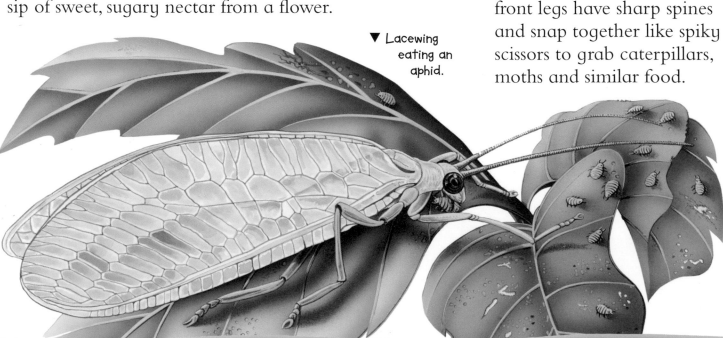

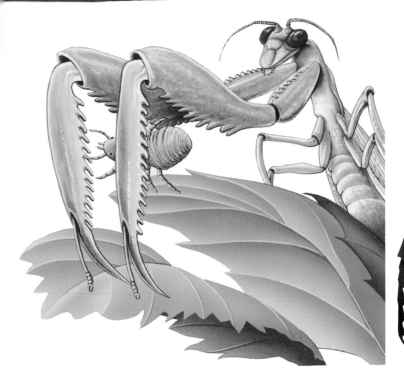

▲ The mantis stays perfectly still, camouflaged by its body coloring which blends in with the leaf or flower where it waits. When a victim comes near—SNAP!

41

Ant lions are insects that resemble lacewings. The ant lion larva lives in sand or loose soil. It digs a small pit and then hides below the surface at the bottom. Small creatures wander past, slip and slide into the pit, and the ant lion larva grasps them with its fanglike mouthparts.

▲ The ant lion larva sits in a small hole at the bottom of its pit, waiting for an unwary ant.

Veggie bugs

42 About 9 out of 10 kinds of insects eat some kind of plant food. Many feed on soft, rich, nutritious substances. These include the sap in stems and leaves, the mineral-rich liquid in roots, the nectar in flowers, and the soft flesh of squashy fruits and berries.

43 Solid wood may not seem very tasty, but many kinds of insects eat it. They usually consume the wood when they are larvae or grubs, making tunnels as they eat their way through trees, logs, and wood structures such as bridges, fences, houses, and furniture.

Elm beetle

Elm beetle larva

Furniture beetle

Woodworm (Furniture beetle larva)

Flowerbug

Mealy-bug

44 Insects even feed on old bits of damp and crumbling wood, dying trees, brown and decaying leaves, and smelly, rotting fruit. They are not fussy eaters! This is nature's way of recycling nutrients in old plant parts, and returning them to the soil so new trees and other plants can grow.

Capsid bug

Shield bug

Fruitfly

Lacebug

I DON'T BELIEVE IT!

Animal droppings are delicious and tasty to many kinds of insects. Various types of beetles lay their eggs in warm and steamy piles of droppings. The larvae soon hatch out and eat the dung!

Unwelcome guests

45 Insects may be small, but some have very powerful bites and poison stingers. A few can even kill people. The hornet is a large type of wasp and has a jagged sting on its rear end. It does not use this often. But when it does, it can cause great pain to a person and easily kill a small animal.

◀ Hornet

Hornet's stinger

▶ Bee

— Bee's stinger

46 Like wasps, bees also have a poison stinger at their rear end. After the wasp jabs its stinger into an enemy, the stinger comes out and the wasp can fly away and use it again. It's like stabbing with a dagger. But when a bee does this, the stinger has a hook or barb and stays in the enemy. As the bee flies away the rear part of its body tears off and the bee soon dies.

47 **Bird—eating spiders really do eat birds!** They inject their venom, or poison, into their prey with large fangs. As well as birds, they eat lizards, frogs, and even small poisonous snakes. It can take as much as a day to suck the body of a snake dry!

▲ Bombardier beetle

48 **The bombardier beetle squirts out a spray of horrible liquid from its rear end, almost like a small spray gun!** This startles and stings the attacker and gives the small beetle time to escape.

QUIZ

Do you know which of these insects is most poisonous or harmful to a person, and which is the least dangerous?

Hornet
Grasshopper
Bee

Earwig
Bulldog ant
Moth

From the most to least dangerous: hornet (powerful stinger), bee (less powerful stinger), bulldog ant (stinging bite), moth (a few types have stinging hairs on the body), grasshopper (might scratch when it kicks) earwig (pretty much totally harmless)

49 **One army ant can give a small bite.** But 10,000 are much more dangerous. These ants are mainly from South America and do not stay in a nest like other ants. They crawl in long lines through the forest, eating whatever they can bite, sting and overpower, from other insects to large spiders, lizards, and birds. They rest at night before marching on the next day.

Towns for termites

50 Some insects live together in huge groups called colonies—which are like insect cities. There are four main types of insects which form colonies. One is the termites. The other three are all in the same insect subgroup and are bees, wasps, and ants.

51 Some kinds of termites make their nests inside a huge pile of mud and earth called a termite mound. The termites build the mound from wet mud which goes hard in the hot sun. The main part of the nest is below ground level. It has hundreds of tunnels and chambers where the termites live, feed and breed.

▶ Termites mounds are incredibly complex constructions. They can reach 33 feet (10 meters) tall, and have air-conditioning shafts built into them. These enable the termites to control the temperature of the nest to within 1 degree.

52 Inside the termite "city" there are various groups of termites, with different kinds of work to do. Some tunnel into the soil and collect food such as tiny bits of plants. Others guard the entrance to the nest and bite any animals which try to enter. Some look after the eggs and young forms, or larvae.

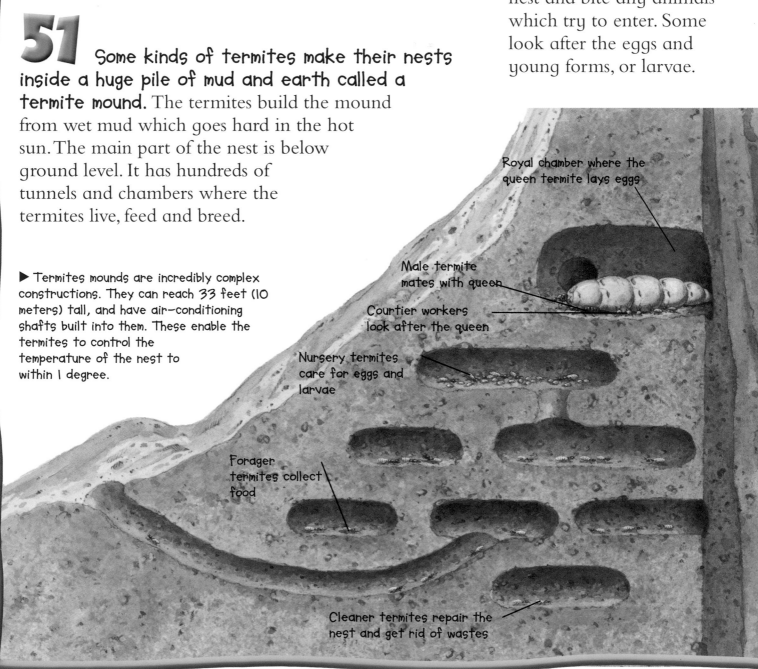

Royal chamber where the queen termite lays eggs

Male termite mates with queen

Courtier workers look after the queen

Nursery termites care for eggs and larvae

Forager termites collect food

Cleaner termites repair the nest and get rid of wastes

55
A wasp nest will have about 2,000 wasps in it, but these are small builders in the insect world! A termite colony may have more than 5,000,000 inhabitants! Other insect colonies are smaller, although most have a similar setup with one queen and various kinds of workers. Wood ants form nests of up to 300,000 and honeybees around 50,000. Some bumblebees live in colonies numbering only 10 or 20.

53
The queen termite is up to 100 times bigger than the workers. She is the only one in the nest who lays eggs—thousands every day.

54
Leaf—cutter ants grow their own food! They harvest leaves which they use at the nest to grow fungus, which they eat.

I DON'T BELIEVE IT!
Ants get milk from green cows! The "cows" are really aphids. Ants look after the aphids. In return, when an ant strokes an aphid, the aphid oozes a drop of "milk," a sugary liquid called honeydew, which the ant sips to get energy.

▲ When the sections of leaf are taken back to the nest, other ants cut them up into smaller sections. They are then used in gardens to grow the ants' food.

Where am I?

56 Insects have some of the best types of camouflage in the whole world of animals. Camouflage is when a living thing is colored and patterned to blend in with its surroundings, so it is difficult to notice. This makes it hard for predators to see or find it. Or, if the insect is a predator itself, camouflage helps it to creep up unnoticed on prey.

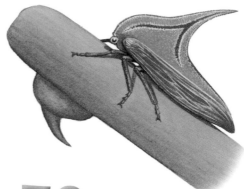

58 The thornbug has a hard, pointed body casing. It sits still on a twig pretending to be a real thorn. It moves around and feeds at night.

57 Stick and leaf insects look exactly like sticks and leaves. The body and legs of a stick insect are long and twiglike. The body of a leaf insect has wide, flat parts which are colored to resemble leaves. Both these types of insects eat plants. When the wind blows they rock and sway in the breeze, just like the real twigs and leaves around them.

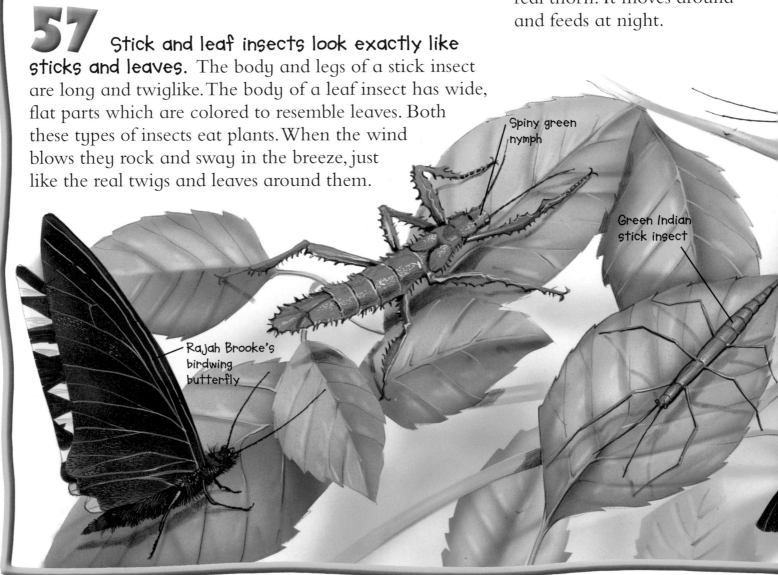

Spiny green nymph

Green Indian stick insect

Rajah Brooke's birdwing butterfly

59 Shieldbugs have broad, flat bodies that look like the leaves around them. The body is shaped like the shield carried by a medieval knight-in-armor.

60 Many butterflies seem too brightly colored to blend in with their surroundings. But when the wings are held together over the butterfly's back, the undersides show. These are usually brown or green—dark colors like the leaves.

Green Indian stick insect

Rajah Brooke's birdwing butterfly

MAKE A CAMOUFLAGE SCENE

1. Carefully cut out a butterfly shape from cardboard. Color it brightly with a bold pattern, such as yellow and brown spots on an orange background, or orange stripes on a blue background.

2. Cut out 10–20 leaf shapes from cardboard. Color them like your butterfly. Stick the leaves on a cardboard branch.

3. Your butterfly may seem far too bright and bold to be camouflaged. But put the butterfly on your branch. See how well its camouflage works now!

61 The bird-dropping caterpillar looks just like—a pile of bird's droppings! Not many animals would want to eat it, so it survives longer.

31

Great pretenders

62 Some insects pretend to be what they're not—especially other insects. For example, a hoverfly has a body with yellow and black stripes. At first sight it looks very similar to a wasp. But it is not. It is a type of fly and it is harmless. It cannot sting like a real wasp.

63 A mimic is an animal that, at a glance, looks similar to another animal, but which is really a different kind of creature. The animal which the mimic resembles is known as the model. Usually, the model is dangerous or harmful in some way. It may have a powerful bite or a poisonous sting. Other animals avoid it. Usually, the mimic is harmless. But it looks like the harmful model, so other animals avoid it too. The mimic gains safety or protection by looking like the model.

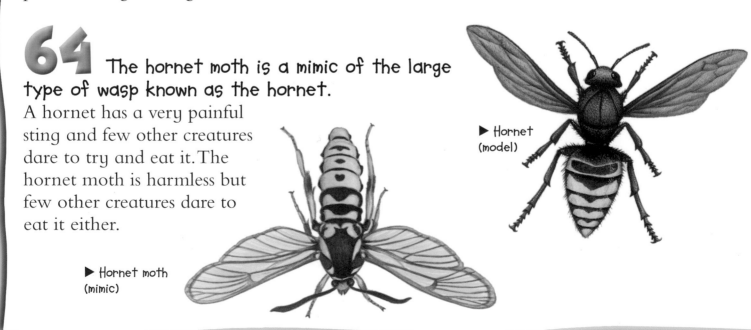

▲ The harmless hoverfly looks just like a wasp. Like other mimics, it fools other animals into thinking that it is more dangerous than it is.

64 The hornet moth is a mimic of the large type of wasp known as the hornet. A hornet has a very painful sting and few other creatures dare to try and eat it. The hornet moth is harmless but few other creatures dare to eat it either.

► Hornet (model)

► Hornet moth (mimic)

65 **The monarch butterfly has bright, bold colors on its wings.** These warn other animals, such as birds and lizards, that its flesh tastes horrible and is poisonous. The viceroy butterfly is very similar to the monarch but it is a mimic—its flesh is not distasteful. As well as being poisonous, the monarch is also a champion migrating insect.

Monarch butterfly

Viceroy butterfly

66 **The bee fly cannot sting like a real bee.** But it looks just like a bee, with a hairy striped body.

The bee fly avoids predators by looking like a bee.

67 **The ant beetle resembles an ant,** although it does not have a strong bite and a sting like a real ant. The ant beetle enters the ant's nest and steals ant larvae to eat.

QUIZ

Sort these models and mimics into pairs where the harmless mimic looks like the harmful model.

Mimic	Model
Ant beetle	Hornet
Bee fly	Ant
Hornet moth	Bee
Hoverfly	Monarch
Viceroy	Wasp

Ant beetle and ant; bee fly and bee; Hornet moth and hornet, hoverfly and wasp; viceroy and monarch.

Stay or go?

68 The cold of winter or the dryness of drought are hard times for most animals, including insects. How can they survive? One answer is to hibernate. Many insects find a safe, sheltered place and go to sleep. Butterflies crawl behind creepers and vines. Ladybugs cluster in thick bushes. Beetles dig into the soil or among tree roots. However, these insects are not really asleep in the way that you go to sleep. They are simply too cold to move. As the weather becomes warmer, they become active again.

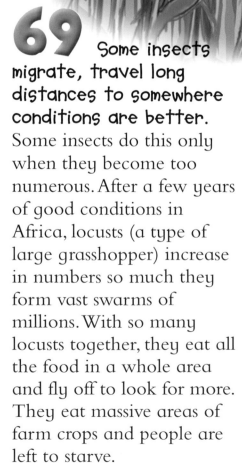

69 Some insects migrate, travel long distances to somewhere conditions are better. Some insects do this only when they become too numerous. After a few years of good conditions in Africa, locusts (a type of large grasshopper) increase in numbers so much they form vast swarms of millions. With so many locusts together, they eat all the food in a whole area and fly off to look for more. They eat massive areas of farm crops and people are left to starve.

Peacock butterfly

Ladybug

Squash beetle

▲ All these insects hibernate through winter each year.

I DON'T BELIEVE IT!

Some insects migrate the wrong way! In Australia bogong moths sometimes fly off in search of better conditions. Some keep on flying out over the sea, fall into the water and die.

70

Some insects migrate every year. In North America, monarch butterflies fly south during autumn. They spend the winter in warm parts of California, and Mexico. Millions of monarchs gather there in winter roosts. Next spring they fly north again to feed and breed.

71

Some insects migrate every year. These include ladybugs, death's head hawkmoths, painted lady butterflies, and libellula dragonflies.

Death's head hawkmoth

Noisy neighbors

72 The tropical forest is warm and still—but far from quiet. Many insects are making chirps, buzzes, clicks, screeches, hums, and other noises. Most are males, making their songs or calls to attract females at breeding time.

73 Some of the noisiest insects are cicadas, plant-eating bugs with large wings. The male cicada has two thin patches of body casing, one on either side of its abdomen (rear body part). Tiny muscles pull in each patch, then let it go again, like clicking a tin lid in and out. This happens very fast and the clicks merge into a buzzing sound which can be heard for half a mile (800 meters).

Giant wood wasp

Great green bush cricket

Mole cricket

Cicada

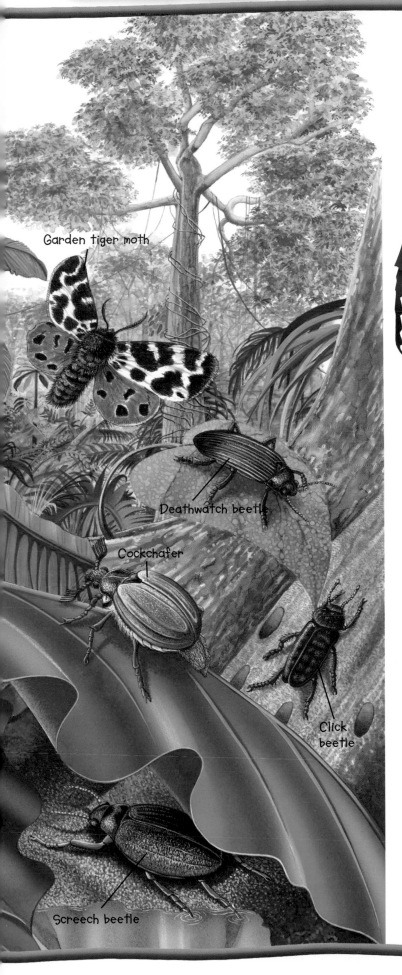

Garden tiger moth

Deathwatch beetle

Cockchafer

Click beetle

Screech beetle

74 **Like most other crickets, the male katydid chirps by rubbing together his wings.** The bases of the wings near the body have hard, ridged strips like rows of pegs. These click past each other to make the chirping sound.

75 **The male mole cricket chirps in a similar way.** But he also sits at the entrance to his burrow in the soil. (Mole crickets get their name from the way they tunnel through soil, like real moles.) The burrow entrance is specially shaped, almost like the loudspeaker of a music system. It makes the chirps sound louder and travel farther.

Meet the family!

76 Are all minibeasts, bugs and creepy-crawlies truly insects?
One way to tell is to count the legs. If a creature has six legs, it's an insect. If it has fewer or more, it's some other kind of animal. However, leg-counting only works with fully grown or adult creatures. Some young forms or larvae, like fly maggots, have no legs at all. But they develop into six-legged flies, and flies are certainly insects.

Maggots

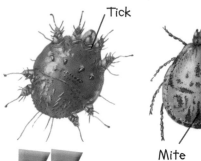

Tick

Mite

77 Mites and ticks have eight legs. They are not insects. Ticks and some mites cling onto larger animals and suck their blood. Some mites are so small that a handful of soil may contain half a million of them. Mites and ticks belong to the group of animals with eight legs, called arachnids. Other arachnids are spiders and scorpions.

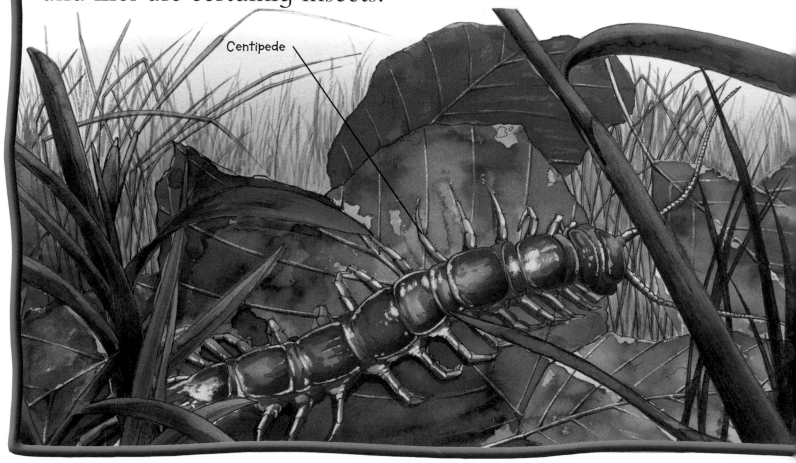

Centipede

78 A woodlouse has a hard body casing and feelers on its head. But it has more than 10 legs so it is certainly not an insect! It is a crustacean— a cousin of crabs and lobsters.

79 Centipedes have lots of legs, far more than six—usually more than 30. The centipede has two very long fangs that give a poison bite. It races across the ground hunting for small animals to eat—such as insects.

80 Millipedes have 50 or 100 legs, maybe even more. They are certainly not insects. Millipedes eat bits of plants such as old leaves, bark, and wood.

QUIZ

Which of these minibeasts has a poisonous bite or sting?

Millipede
Scorpion
Woodlouse
Tick
Centipede
Maggot

Only the centipede and scorpion have a poisonous bite or sting.

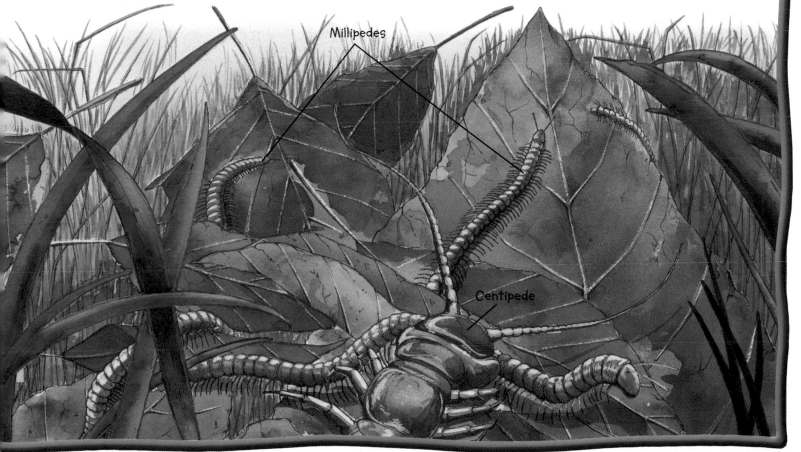

Millipedes

Centipede

Silky spiders

81 **A spider has eight legs.** So it's not an insect. It's a type of animal called an arachnid. All spiders are deadly hunters. They have large fanglike jaws which they use to grab and stab their prey. The fangs inject a poison to kill or quiet the victim. The spider then tears it apart and eats it, or sucks out its body juices. Like spiders, scorpions and mites and ticks have eight legs. So they are also arachnids.

Several spinnerets produce silk

Spigots produce coarse silk for making webs

Spools produce fine silk for wrapping prey

82 **All spiders can make very thin, fine threads called silk.** These come out of the rear of the spider's body, from parts called spinnerets. Spiders spin their silk for many reasons. About half of the 40,000 different kinds of spiders make webs or nets to catch prey. Some spiders wrap up their living victims in silk to stop them escaping, so the spider can have its meal later. Some female spiders make silk bags, called cocoons, where they lay their eggs, and others spin protective silk "nursery tents" for their babies.

▼ A spider starts a web by building a bridge.

▲ Then it makes a triangle shape.

▼ It adds more threads to make a strong framework.

▲ Finally, the spider fills the frame with circular threads.

▼ A spider's web is strong enough to catch large insects.

◄ The Australian redback spider is one of the most deadly of a group called widow spiders. These spiders get their name because, once they have mated, the female may well eat the male!

MAKE A SPIDER'S WEB

You will need

a piece of cardboard   a spool of thread
round-ended scissors   glue or tape

1. Ask an adult for help. Cut a large hole out of the cardboard. Stretch some thread across the hole and glue or tape both ends.

2. Do the same again several times at a different angles. Make sure all the threads cross at the center of the hole.

3. Starting at the center, glue a long piece of thread to one of the cross pieces, then to the next cross piece but slightly farther away from the center, and so on. Work your way around in a growing spiral until you reach the edge. That's the way that real spiders make webs.

83 Some spiders have very strange ways of using their silk threads. The spitting spider squirts sticky silk at its victim, like throwing tiny ropes over it. The bolas spider catches moths and other insects flying past with its own kind of fishing line. The water spider makes a crisscross sheet of silk that holds bubbles of air. It brings the air down from the surface, so the spider can breathe underwater.

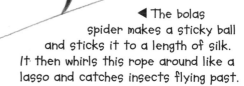

◄ The bolas spider makes a sticky ball and sticks it to a length of silk. It then whirls this rope around like a lasso and catches insects flying past.

Inventive arachnids

84 Not all spiders catch their prey using webs. Wolf spiders are strong and have long legs. They run fast and chase tiny prey such as beetles, caterpillars, and slugs.

▲ Wolf spider

86 The trapdoor spider lives in a burrow with a wedge-shaped door made from silk. The spider hides just behind this door. When it detects a small animal passing, it opens the door and rushes out to grab its victim.

▶ This gold leaf crab spider has caught a honeybee. Its venom works fast to paralyze the bee. If it did not, the bee's struggling might harm the spider and draw the attention of the spider's enemies.

85 The crab spider looks like a small crab, with a wide, tubby body and curved legs. It usually sits on a flower which is the same color as itself. It keeps very still so it is camouflaged—it merges in with its surroundings. Small animals such as flies, beetles, and bees come to the flower to gather food and the crab spider pounces on them.

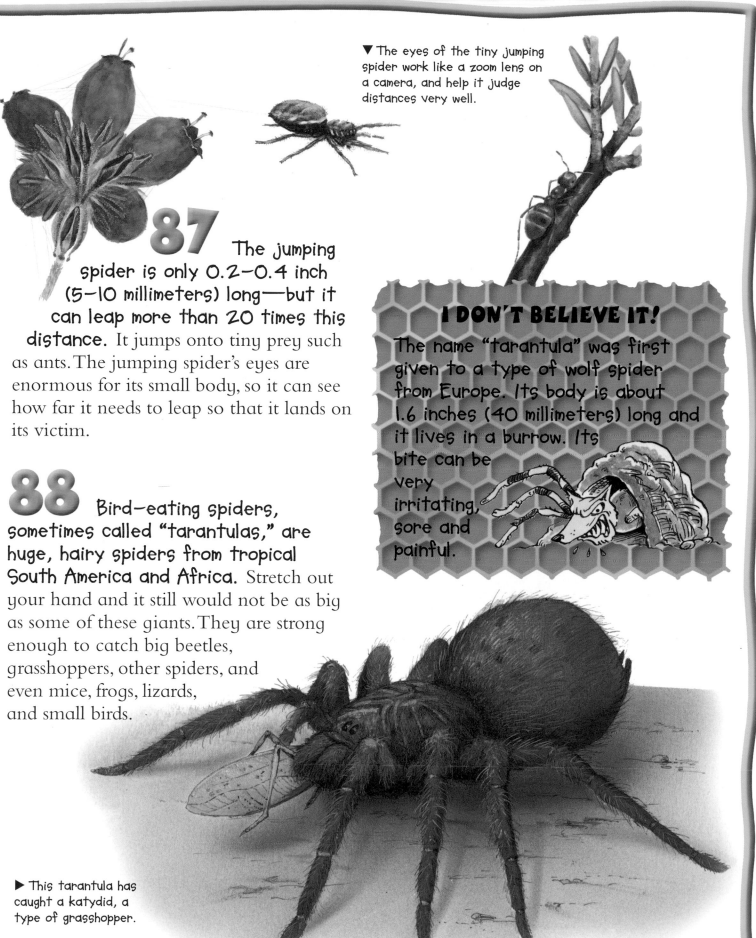

▼ The eyes of the tiny jumping spider work like a zoom lens on a camera, and help it judge distances very well.

87
The jumping spider is only 0.2–0.4 inch (5–10 millimeters) long—but it can leap more than 20 times this distance. It jumps onto tiny prey such as ants. The jumping spider's eyes are enormous for its small body, so it can see how far it needs to leap so that it lands on its victim.

88
Bird-eating spiders, sometimes called "tarantulas," are huge, hairy spiders from tropical South America and Africa. Stretch out your hand and it still would not be as big as some of these giants. They are strong enough to catch big beetles, grasshoppers, other spiders, and even mice, frogs, lizards, and small birds.

I DON'T BELIEVE IT!
The name "tarantula" was first given to a type of wolf spider from Europe. Its body is about 1.6 inches (40 millimeters) long and it lives in a burrow. Its bite can be very irritating, sore and painful.

▶ This tarantula has caught a katydid, a type of grasshopper.

A sting in the tail

89 A scorpion has eight legs. It is not an insect. Like a spider, it is an arachnid. Scorpions live in warm parts of the world. Some are at home in dripping rain forests. Others like baking deserts. The scorpion has large, crab-like pincers, called pedipalps, to grab its prey, and powerful jaws like scissors to chop it up.

90 The scorpion has a dangerous poison sting at the tip of its tail. It may use this to poison or paralyze a victim, so the victim cannot move. Or the scorpion may wave its tail at enemies to warn them that, unless they go away, it will sting them to death!

▶ This scorpion has caught a katydid. It has paralyzed it with its sting, and will soon settle down to eat.

91 The sun spider or solifuge is another very fierce, eight-legged, spiderlike hunter, with a poisonous bite. It lives in deserts and dry places, which is why it's sometimes called the camel spider.

92 The false scorpion looks like a scorpion, with big pincers. But it does not have a poisonous sting in its tail. It doesn't even have a tail. And it's tiny—it could fit into this "o"! It lives in the soil and hunts even smaller creatures.

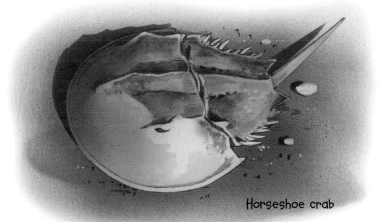

Horseshoe crab

93 A crab may seem an odd cousin for a spider or scorpion. But the horseshoe or king crab is very unusual. It has eight legs—so it's an arachnid. It also has a large domed shell and strong spiky tail. There were horseshoe crabs in the seas well before dinosaurs roamed the land.

QUIZ

Look though this book and decide which of these animals are NOT insects. How can you tell—by counting the legs? Not always!

Beetle   Millipede
Caterpillar   Scorpion
Cricket   Scorpionfly
King crab   Slug
Louse   Tarantula

They are all insects apart from the king crab, millipede, scorpion, slug, and the tarantula

94 Animals don't have to be big to be dangerous. These spiders are both very poisonous and their bites can even kill people. This is why you should never fool around with spiders or poke your hands into holes and dark places!

Violin spider

Black widow spider

Friends and foes

95 Some insects are harmful— but others are very helpful. They are a vital part of the natural world. Flies, butterflies, beetles, and many others visit flowers to collect nectar and pollen to eat. In the process they carry pollen from flower to flower. This is called pollination and is needed so that the flower can form seeds or fruits.

96 Spiders are very helpful to gardeners. They catch lots of insect pests, like flies, in their webs.

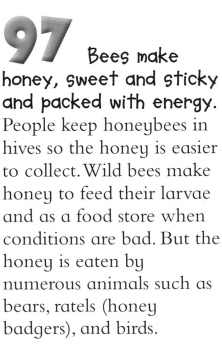

97 Bees make honey, sweet and sticky and packed with energy. People keep honeybees in hives so the honey is easier to collect. Wild bees make honey to feed their larvae and as a food store when conditions are bad. But the honey is eaten by numerous animals such as bears, ratels (honey badgers), and birds.

◄ These bees are busy working in their hive. On the right you can see the young, c-shaped grubs.

98

A few kinds of insects are among the most harmful creatures in the world. They do not attack and kill people directly, like tigers and crocodiles. But they do spread many types of dangerous diseases such as malaria.

99

Blood-sucking flies bite a person with a certain disease, such as malaria, and suck in a small amount of blood. This contains millions of microscopic germs which cause the disease. As the fly bites another person, a tiny drop of the first person's blood gets into the second person— and the disease is passed on.

100

Some insects even damage wooden houses, bridges, barns, and walkways. Certain kinds of termites make nests in the wood and tunnel inside it. The damage cannot be seen from the outside until the wood is eaten almost hollow. Then it collapses into a pile of dust if anyone even touches it!

Index